BEING
TRANSGENDER

Other Books in the LIVING PROUD! Series

Coming Out and Seeking Support

Confronting Stereotypes

Engaging with Politics

Facing Homophobia

Finding Community

Keeping Physically Healthy

Living with Religion and Faith

Staying Mentally Healthy

Understanding Sexual Orientation and Gender Identity

LIVING PROUD! GROWING UP LGBTQ

BEING TRANSGENDER

Robert Rodi and Laura Ross

Foreword by Kevin Jennings
Founder, GLSEN (the Gay, Lesbian & Straight
Education Network)

MASON CREST

Mason Crest
450 Parkway Drive, Suite D
Broomall, PA 19008
www.masoncrest.com

Printed in the United States of America

First printing
9 8 7 6 5 4 3 2 1

Series ISBN: 978-1-4222-3501-0
Hardcover ISBN: 978-1-4222-3502-7
ebook ISBN: 978-1-4222-8375-2

Cataloging-in-Publication Data is available on file at the Library of Congress.

Developed and Produced by Print Matters Productions, Inc. (www.printmattersinc.com)
Cover and Interior Design by Kris Tobiassen, Matchbook Digital

Picture credits: 10, KaninRoman/iStock; 12, Kais Tolmats/iStock; 18, Syda Productions/Shutterstock; 20, DegasMM/iStock; 22, Richee, E.R./Newscom/Album; 26, Zooropa/Fotolia; 28, Karen Struthers/ Fotolia; 31, lev radin/Shutterstock; 35, Achels/Fotolia; 37, kutena/Shutterstock; 41, TransActive; 44, Izumi Hasegawa/Hollywood News Wire/Newscom; 46, Monica Helms/Wikimedia Commons; 47, PR Photos; 49, Vanity Fair/ZUMA Press/Newscom; 53, Diana Mrazikova/ZUMA Press/Newscom
Front cover: ibeklaus/iStock: trail to the Flatirons, Boulder, Colorado

BEING TRANSGENDER

CONTENTS

Foreword by Kevin Jennings, Founder, GLSEN 8

1 What Is Gender? 11

Sex ≠ Gender 13

Close-up: Sex versus Gender 14

Gender Roles and Sexuality 15

The Myth of the "Real Man" 16

Close-up: The Roots of Gender Prejudice 17

Gender Roles: Still Evolving 18

Close-up: Gender Programming from Birth 20

2 What Is Transgender? 23

The Wide Range of Gender Variance 25

Crossdressers and Drag Performers 27

Close-up: Intersex—Born Both Male and Female 28

Transitioning from Male to Female or Female to Male 29

Transgender ≠ Gay 30

3 Growing Up Transgender 33

Hormone Therapy to Redirect Puberty 34

Too Young to Be Certain? 36

Parental Concern … and Confusion 38

The Risks of Repressing Gender Identity 40

Close-up: Finding a Trans Community 42

4 Living as a Transgender Adult 45

The Downside of Acceptance 48

Changing the Way We Think About Transgender Individuals 51

Close-up: Gender-neutral Pronouns 52

Worth the Ongoing Struggle 53

Glossary 56

Further Resources 62

Index 64

KEY ICONS TO LOOK FOR

Text-Dependent Questions: These questions send the reader back to the text for a closer look at the evidence presented there.

Words to Understand: These words and their easy-to-understand definitions will increase the reader's understanding of the text while building vocabulary skills.

Series Glossary of Key Terms: This back-of-the-book glossary contains terminology used throughout this series. Words found here increase the reader's ability to read and comprehend higher-level books and articles in this field.

Research Projects: Readers are pointed toward areas of further inquiry connected to each chapter. Suggestions are provided for projects that encourage deeper research and analysis.

Sidebars: This boxed material within the main text allows readers to build knowledge, gain insights, explore possibilities, and cultivate realistic and holistic perspectives.

FOREWORD

I loved libraries as a kid.

Every Saturday my mom and I would drive from the trailer where we lived on an unpaved road in the unincorporated town of Lewisville, North Carolina, and make the long drive to the "big city" of Winston-Salem to go to the downtown public library, where I would spend joyous hours perusing the books on the shelves. I'd end up lugging home as many books as my arms could carry and generally would devour them over the next seven days, all the while eagerly anticipating next week's trip. The library opened up all kinds of worlds to me—all kinds of worlds, except a gay one.

Oh, I found some "gay" books, even in the dark days of the 1970s. I'm not sure how I did, but I found my way to authors like Tennessee Williams, Yukio Mishima, and Gore Vidal. While these great artists created masterpieces of literature that affirmed that there were indeed other gay people in the universe, their portrayals of often-doomed gay men hardly made me feel hopeful about my future. It was better than nothing, but not much better. I felt so lonely and isolated I attempted to take my own life my junior year of high school.

In the 35 years since I graduated from high school in 1981, much has changed. Gay–straight alliances (an idea my students and I pioneered at Concord Academy in 1988) are now widespread in American schools. Out LGBT (lesbian, gay, bisexual, and transgender) celebrities and programs with LGBT themes are commonplace on the airwaves. Oregon has a proud bisexual governor, multiple members of Congress are out as lesbian, gay, or bisexual, and the White House was bathed in rainbow colors the day marriage equality became the law of the land in 2015. It gets better, indeed.

So why do we need the Living Proud! series?

- Because GLSEN (the Gay, Lesbian & Straight Education Network) reports that over two-thirds of LGBT students routinely hear anti-LGBT language at school.

- Because GLSEN reports that over 60% of LGBT students do not feel safe at school.
- Because the CDC (the Centers for Disease Control and Prevention, a U.S. government agency) reports that lesbian and gay students are four times more likely to attempt suicide than heterosexual students.

In my current role as the executive director of the Arcus Foundation (the world's largest financial supporter of LGBT rights), I work in dozens of countries and see how far there still is to go. In over 70 countries same-sex relations are crimes under existing laws: in 8, they are a crime punishable by the death penalty. It's better, but it's not all better—especially in our libraries, where there remains a need for books that address LGBT issues that are appropriate for young people, books that will erase both the sense of isolation so many young LGBT people still feel as well as the ignorance so many non-LGBT young people have, ignorance that leads to the hate and violence that still plagues our community, both at home and abroad.

The Living Proud! series will change that and will save lives. By providing accurate, age-appropriate information to young people of all sexual orientations and gender identities, the Living Proud! series will help young people understand the complexities of the LGBT experience. Young LGBT people will see themselves in its pages, and that reflection will help them see a future full of hope and promise. I wish Living Proud! had been on the shelves of the Winston-Salem/Forsyth County Public Library back in the seventies. It would have changed my life. I'm confident that it will have as big an impact on its readers today as it would have had on me back then. And I commend it to readers of any age.

Kevin Jennings
Founder, GLSEN (the Gay, Lesbian & Straight Education Network)
Executive Director, Arcus Foundation

GLSEN®

GLSEN is the leading national education organization focused on ensuring safe and affirming schools for all students. GLSEN seeks to develop school climates where difference is valued for the positive contribution it makes to creating a more vibrant and diverse community.
www.glsen.org

The opening of traditionally masculine jobs, such as soldiers in the military, has had a profound effect on how people view gender.

1.
WHAT IS GENDER?

 WORDS TO UNDERSTAND

Normative: Behavior that is considered normal and acceptable.
Effeminate: A man who is seen as having feminine characteristics.
Binary: A system made up of two, and only two, parts.
Ambiguity: Something unclear or confusing.

Most people are assumed to be either male or female at birth. And up until very recently in our culture, that single accident of birth directed the rest of a person's life. From how they dressed, played, and were educated to possible jobs, careers, and life partners, a person's assigned birth gender defined to a huge extent society's expectations and the opportunities open to them.

We can tell immediately which doll is Barbie and which is Ken. Barbie has a pink dress, long hair, and high-heeled shoes. Ken sports short hair, is dressed all in blue, and wears flat shoes. These are all gender characteristics our culture has assigned to the biological sexes.

Midway through the last century, things began to change. More and more women chose traditionally "masculine" careers as doctors or police officers, while men—in fewer numbers, but still significantly—put on lipstick and eyeliner to sing in rock-and-roll bands, or found happiness as stay-at-home dads. There was, as might be expected, some strong criticism of this new trend of women who behaved like men and men who feminized themselves; however, by the beginning of the 21st century, the formerly rigid gender roles people had been forced to live by had become much more elastic.

Although it's true that many boys and girls still fall into those original gender roles naturally, it no longer surprises us when they don't. We see pint-sized boy princesses at our doors on Halloween and women vying for active combat positions in the military. We are starting to understand that gender is a more complex matter than just what "plumbing" we are born with.

For a long time, we used the terms *sex* and *gender* interchangeably, as if they meant the same thing. Clearly, they don't.

Sex ≠ Gender

In fact, there is no biological basis for the way we are accustomed to viewing gender roles. There's nothing about an individual's sex that drives his or her behavior. Women aren't required to love flowers and lace simply because they're biologically female, and men aren't compelled to enjoy sports and cars. The term *gender nonconforming* refers to breaking away from traditional gender roles—in other words, declining to fulfill the roles traditionally associated with the gender you were assigned at birth.

"While gender identities are internal to a person, gender roles are handed to us by society," says Dr. Laura Erickson-Schroth, who studies transgender health issues. "We should be teaching our children that whatever bodies they live in, they can choose to reject gender roles. For some gender-nonconforming people, it feels right to live in the bodies into which they are born, but to challenge gender-**normative** behaviors."

Although we've certainly made progress in that direction, we still have a long way to go. In America, gender-nonconforming women are everywhere, but gender-nonconforming men ... not so much.

 CLOSE-UP: SEX VERSUS GENDER

Many people assume that *gender* and *sexuality* mean the same thing, but they are actually two different concepts. According to the World Health Organization:

- *Sex* refers to the biological and physiological characteristics that define men and women.
- *Gender* refers to the socially constructed roles, behaviors, activities, and attributes that a society considers appropriate for men and women.

To put it another way: *Male* and *female* are sex categories, whereas *masculine* and *feminine* are gender categories.

   Aspects of sex do not vary substantially among different human societies, but aspects of gender can vary greatly.

Examples of *Sex* Characteristics

- Women menstruate, whereas men do not.
- Men have testicles, whereas women do not.
- Women have breasts that can produce milk, whereas men do not.
- Men generally have heavier bones than women do.

Examples of *Gender* Characteristics

- In the United States (and most other countries), women earn significantly less money than men do for similar work.
- In many countries (including the United States until very recently), women and men are expected to serve different functions in the military—men on the front lines, women in support roles.
- In Saudi Arabia, men are allowed to drive cars, but women are not.
- In many developing nations, men are educated and women are not.
- In most of the world, women do more housework than men do and take on more of the childrearing responsibilities, whereas men are expected to support the family.

Gender Roles and Sexuality

"We live in a time when women can do anything they want," said Carolyn Gierga, a single woman in her thirties who owns her own home and has a thriving career in the medical field. "But it's still different for men. They're expected to be the ones who can fix things. They're expected to be strong and stable. Women do things that men do, and it's perfectly normal. But when men do things that women traditionally do, we think it's weird. Or we assume they're gay!"

For gender-nonconforming males, these traditional roles and rules of society can be very confusing. If a young boy enjoys singing and dancing, or even wearing dresses, it's generally assumed that he's gay. But gender roles aren't necessarily related to sexuality. Just as little girls who are tomboys often grow up to be straight women, little boys who enjoy activities or modes of dress typically associated with girls can still grow up to be straight men.

Researchers Madeline Heilman and Aaron Wallen from New York University and Columbia University, respectively, found that when men succeed in occupations traditionally held by women, they tend to be considered "wimpy" by their co-workers, and are often treated with disrespect. Women who succeed in jobs usually held by men, on the other hand, tend to be admired.

The Myth of the "Real Man"

"So many people assume that **effeminate** men are always gay, and that does a disservice to both gay men and straight men, because it's so limiting," said Helena Barrett, who worked with a transgender advocacy group in Western New York. "Men, much more than women, are told they have to behave a certain way in order to be considered a 'real man.' When you really stop and think about that, it makes no sense at all. And I think it's encouraging that, more and more, people are starting to think about those things. And they realize that we're all a lot happier if we can just be who we are."

But traditions die hard, and we still tend to give babies a push in the direction signified by their sex. When we dress baby boys in blue and baby girls in pink, we are validating a **binary** gender system, meaning that there are just two options for gender—male or female—and that these are dictated by biology. As they grow up, boys and girls who don't feel comfortable with these gender roles will have to struggle to be free of them, and that process can be difficult.

"**Ambiguity** has never been popular," said Rachel Kahn, a student at Bryn Mawr College who researched binary gender systems in sports. "We like to categorize, and we don't like it when people do not fit neatly into our categories."

 CLOSE-UP: THE ROOTS OF GENDER PREJUDICE

Some sociologists are concerned that feminine gender qualities are still being looked down upon in our culture. They point out that the reason it's okay for women to dress and act like men but not okay for men to dress and act like women is that so-called "masculine" behaviors are seen as strong, competent, professional, and admirable. In contrast, "feminine" qualities, such as being nurturing, sensitive, and creative, are regarded as weaker or trivial.

Women may not face the same kinds of discrimination they once did, as long as they can conform to masculine gender roles; however, men who want to push past the boundaries of those same gender roles *do* face discrimination. In other words, sex may no longer be the basis for prejudice and discrimination—but gender still is.

Notice how similarly these male and female businesspeople are dressed. Appropriate clothing for businesswomen is very much the same as that for men. Why should women be expected to dress and act like men in order to be respected in the business world?

Gender Roles: Still Evolving

To summarize what we've been discussing, *gender* is the collection of behaviors and traits that society typically assigns to each sex. Gender roles change when society changes how it regards men and women. For centuries, society considered women to be of less value than men, but as culture progressed, women achieved some basic equalities—such as the rights to vote and to run for office.

"If you look back in history books at the changes that have occurred in our society in the last hundred years, even, there have been so many ways that the roles of men and women have changed and expanded," Barrett says. "It just stands to reason that things will change just as much, if not more, in the next hundred years. It's arrogant for us to think that the way we look at things now is the only way they will ever be. We are constantly moving forward, constantly progressing."

Barrett herself was raised in a strict religion that adhered to very traditional gender roles. She always wore skirts, and her mother ingrained in her that "the purpose of life is to get married and have children." She wasn't encouraged to go to college, and she was urged to live at her parents' house until she was married and ready to move in with a husband.

"I don't think there's anything wrong with behaving that way, but only if that's what someone actually wants," she says. "The problem is that it starts so early, when we're just little kids. We don't know enough to know who we really are yet. So all we can do is follow what people around us say and do, no matter whether or not it actually fits who we are. Would I have worn skirts every day if I had my own choice? I don't know. All I know is that I don't wear them now. Ever. And I know I'm still a woman."

But what about someone born biologically female who abandons skirts in favor of pants and jackets because of not really *identifying* as a woman? What if this person self-identifies as male?

Clearly this goes beyond gender nonconformity. This is known as being *transgender*.

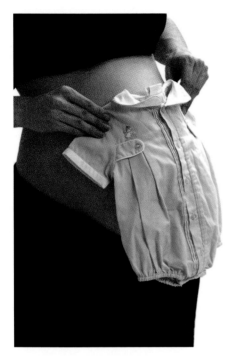 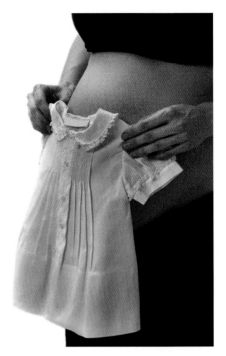

Even before their babies are born, these mothers are shaping gender identities by choosing pink clothes for a girl baby and blue for a boy baby.

 CLOSE-UP: GENDER PROGRAMMING FROM BIRTH

For many parents today, the surprise of finding out whether their child is male or female comes earlier than birth. Although initially used to detect problems prenatally, ultrasound technology is now routinely used to let the parents know whether they'll be having a boy or girl. Once parents, friends, and family members know the child's sex, clothing and toys are purchased, many with a specific gender bias. Even the decorating of the nursery—and certainly the selection of potential names—is influenced by the newborn's sex. These choices begin to set the stage for the development of gender identity in the child, even before that child comes into the world.

Within each culture, and even each family unit, preconceived ideas exist about what it means to be male or female. As soon as the baby is born, the individuals with whom he or she interacts will treat that child as they believe a person of that particular sex should be treated. Parents tend to cuddle and hold female children more than males. Assertive play is often encouraged in male children, whereas females are encouraged to be more gentle. In most cases (though not all, of course), many aspects of the way a baby is treated from the earliest days are based on his or her physical sex.

 ## TEXT-DEPENDENT QUESTIONS

- Can you name some examples of gender characteristics we don't mention in the chapter?
- Why do people dislike gender ambiguity?
- Is gender conformity a religious issue?

 ## RESEARCH PROJECTS

- Make a list of jobs and occupations once reserved for one sex that are now open to both (for instance, flight attendant and garage mechanic).
- Watch an old movie from several decades ago—preferably a romance or romantic comedy. Think about whether the story would be plausible today, with our more flexible gender roles.
- If you're religious, think about ways in which your religion has changed to allow for more diverse gender roles—or has resisted doing so. How do you feel about this?

Movie actress and singer Marlene Dietrich (shown here) flouted gender convention by regularly wearing men's clothes on screen and off in the 1920s and 30s.

2.

WHAT IS TRANSGENDER?

 WORDS TO UNDERSTAND

LGBT: An acronym or abbreviation for lesbian, gay, bisexual, and transgender. Sometimes a "Q" is added (**LGBTQ**) to stand for "questioning," which goes to show how much variation there can be in gender identity. "Q" may also stand for "queer."

Variant: A range of differences within a category such as gender.

Spectrum: A wide range of variations.

Persona: A character or personality portrayed by an actor or entertainer—or just by a person in real life who wants to act like someone else.

Stereotype: A caricature; a way to judge someone, probably unfairly, based on opinions you may have about a particular group they belong to.

Crossdresser ... transvestite ... transsexual ... intersex ... genderqueer ... drag queen ... drag king. All of these are terms used to describe people who dress, behave, or live in a way that eschews traditional notions of gender. The terms are interrelated but not interchangeable, which can be the cause of some confusion. These individuals are often referred to as *transgender.*

"Terminology can be intimidating when you're first learning about anything," says Dr. Laura Erickson-Schroth, who answered questions on transgender issues for readers of the *New York Times*. "And terminology surrounding identities of any kind—racial, sexual, etc.—can be even harder because it changes so rapidly. Even at a given point in time, people within certain groups will disagree about the meaning of terms. Young people have started to shorten the word *transgender* to just *trans*, and this shortened form can mean different things to different people."

Alex Yates, co-president of an **LGBT** activism group at Penn State University, led a student discussion about gender issues. Part of the conversation was aimed at helping people, especially those who do not know any transgender individuals personally, understand potentially confusing terms. Many questions arose about the correct terms to use for people who don't conform to traditional gender roles. He summarized the terminology as simply as he could: "*Transgender* is an umbrella term for any gender-**variant** person." Conversely, *cisgender*—or *cis*—has recently come to be used for people whose gender identity does align with the sex they were assigned at birth.

Being gender-variant means that the way a person thinks about his or her gender doesn't match society's expectations. This may include a strong, masculine woman who fixes cars and wears ties or an effeminate man who enjoys arranging flowers. Or it may be someone who doesn't identify with *either* gender entirely—or even at all. *Gender-variant* may also refer to someone who goes through a surgical change to alter their anatomical sex. Some people refer to gender variance as being "genderqueer."

The Wide Range of Gender Variance

"Some people identify as genderqueer because their gender identity is androgynous," says Erickson-Schroth. "Some use the term *bi-gendered* to describe themselves. Others identify as *nongendered*. Some people use the term *genderqueer* because they oppose the binary gender system."

She recommends the Transsexual Roadmap (tsroadmap.com), an online information resource dealing with transgender issues. It lays out how different people approach what has always been considered a binary gender system: male or female. "*Transsexual,*" she explains, "is an older term that has often been used for individuals who may have had a surgical procedure to reassign their sex. But even if they have not, they still live as a different sex from that which they were assigned at birth. *Transsexual* is now frequently replaced by *transgender.*"

"There is a whole **spectrum** of transgender people, who live their lives in a variety of ways, and that makes it very difficult to define," says Helena Barrett, who has led support groups for friends and families of transgender people. "They even have a hard time understanding themselves. People immediately recognize when they don't fit in with everyone else, but that doesn't mean they can figure out how to fix it or find where they *do* fit. It takes time and understanding."

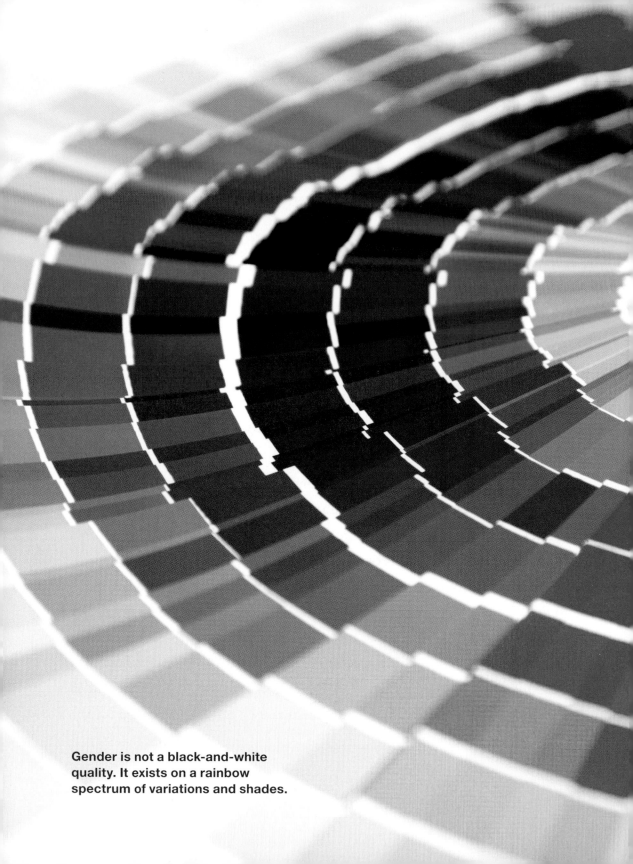

Gender is not a black-and-white quality. It exists on a rainbow spectrum of variations and shades.

Crossdressers and Drag Performers

The word *crossdresser* usually refers to a man who dresses as a woman, also known as a *transvestite*. (Erickson-Schroth explains that although these terms can apply to women who dress as men, they rarely do, "probably because we are more tolerant of women dressing in traditionally male clothing.") She says that crossdressers often dress this way only in certain situations, as opposed to living their entire lives as the opposite sex. In fact, she points out, many identify as straight men.

Drag queens are men who perform as women for entertainment purposes. Similarly, *drag kings* are women who perform as men.

"People who participate in drag often have exciting stage **personas** that exaggerate gender **stereotypes**," Erickson-Schroth explains. "These stage personalities are separate from their own gender identities, which are often in line with their assigned genders."

In other words, a man who performs as a drag queen probably still lives and dresses as a man in his daily life, fulfilling a traditional male gender role. For such people, gender identity is fluid, even playful—whereas for others, it is something vitally central to who they are. Both conditions represent equally valid expressions of gender variance. "When people have the opportunity to learn about their gender identity and to explore who they really are," says Erickson-Schroth, "they can find what works best for them. There are many ways that families and friends can support that. And the more research that is done, the more people can get the help they need to understand their own gender identity."

A drag queen is a male who dresses and makes himself up as a woman for entertainment purposes.

 CLOSE-UP: INTERSEX—BORN BOTH MALE AND FEMALE

It may surprise you, but some people are born biologically both male and female. Known in the past as *hermaphrodites*, we now call these individuals *intersex*. When babies are born with both male and female biological characteristics, the parents and doctor often immediately choose a preferred gender, and the child is raised based on that decision. However, studies have found that some intersex children ultimately identify as a gender other than the one according to which they were raised.

"Even with evidence of many sexes, we continue to insist on just two," says Erickson-Schroth. "Until recently, physicians attempted to erase intersex people by performing surgery on them in early childhood and insisting that they choose a gender in order to fit in."

Transitioning from Male to Female or Female to Male

For some people, transitioning into a new gender identity is as simple as making a conscious decision. Virginia Charles Prince, who founded the cross-dressing magazine *Transvestia*, writes, "I, at least, know the difference between sex and gender and have simply elected to change the latter and not the former."

But for others, transitioning involves changing both their gender *and* their sex—and this can take years to accomplish. Hormone treatments, psychological counseling and evaluation, and surgery are just part of this complex medical process. "The health industry has really been moving forward to find ways of supporting transgender people and providing the services that are needed," Helena Barrett explains.

In many references and online resources, *transgender* is noted as *TG* and *transsexual* as *TS. Male to female (MTF)* is used to describe someone who was assigned male at birth but identifies as female. *Female to male (FTM)* is someone who was assigned female but identifies as male. Some prefer the term *trans man* for an FTM or *trans woman* for an MTF. And a growing number of mental health professionals, including Erickson-Schroth, are doing research to gain a better understanding of the factors that contribute to issues of gender identity.

"I don't consider being transgender to be a mental health problem itself," Barrett says. "But, just like everyone else, I think transgender people can benefit from working with a mental health professional to understand and deal with their emotions and the pressures and stress that can come from resolving gender identity issues."

Transgender ≠ Gay

All of these examples illustrate the complicated ways in which gender identity differs from sexual orientation. Someone who is transgender isn't necessarily gay. And even the meaning of *gay* and *straight* can be confusing. For instance, a trans man—assigned female at birth but living as a man—who is attracted to women most often identifies as straight.

"It can be challenging to be in a relationship with a transgender person," said Barrett, who was involved in a long-term relationship with a trans man. "Before we got together, I considered myself a lesbian. And he would get really upset about that, because even though he was still biologically a female, he identified as a guy. So according to him, that made both of us straight, because we were a man and a woman in a relationship. At the end of the day, those are really just labels. But it made a difference, because the way other people see us really affects the way we see ourselves. So, if people thought of us as a lesbian couple, then it took away from his identity or his feeling of being a man."

Considering all of the questions and the opportunities for confusion, many people are concerned about how to properly address someone who identifies as transgender. Dr. Erickson-Schroth gives some very simple

Janet Mock, a prominent human rights advocate, wrote the *New York Times* bestseller *Redefining Realness: My Path to Womanhood, Identity, Love, & So Much More.*

advice for those situations. "I encourage you to ask the people who you speak with how they identify," she says. "It is their opinion that matters, after all."

Perhaps most important is to ask young children who demonstrate gender nonconformity about how they see themselves. All growing children struggle with sexuality and identity; the struggle of transgender children is exponentially greater.

 TEXT-DEPENDENT QUESTIONS

- Is there a difference between "gender-variant" and "transgender"?
- "Transvestite" and "transsexual" are terms for different kinds of gender nonconformity; which can be considered transgender?
- What part does homosexuality play in gender variance?
- Is a relationship with a trans person a gay relationship?

RESEARCH PROJECTS

- Look at the clothes you're wearing. Consider how they express your gender identity and what they might signal to others.
- Flip through a fashion magazine. Look for elements of crossdressing that have become mainstream (such as jackets and ties for women, handbags for men).
- List some gender-variant celebrities (gay or straight), and ask yourself how that fact affects their careers, popularity, and how they are perceived. Did it help or hurt them to have "come out" about who they are? Should that matter?

3.
GROWING UP TRANSGENDER

 WORDS TO UNDERSTAND

Endocrinologist: A medical doctor who specializes in the treatment of hormonal diseases and disorders.
Hormones: Natural chemical substances produced in the body that influence growth and sexual development.
Trauma: A deeply upsetting or disturbing experience.

At about two years old, Armand put on an old Minnie Mouse dress and refused to take it off.

According to Armand's mother, "it was like, 'NO!' Feet in a stance, a strong stance, just standing there . . . She pretty much from that point on slept in it, stayed in it all day."

National Public Radio featured a story on Armand and her family. To respect the family's privacy, they did not reveal their last name. The family spoke openly about how Armand struggled with gender identity.

Though Armand was designated male at birth, by the time the piece aired several years later, both parents referred to their child as "she." They tried to convince Armand to wear girls' clothing only while in the house, out of fear of what neighbors would say, but Armand's will was too strong. There were frequent tantrums, outbursts, and general unhappiness. Her parents sought medical advice and were given all sorts of diagnoses and treatments—but nothing seemed to help.

Finally, they found a psychologist who told them that Armand had gender identity disorder, a term that has been used for individuals who experience a conflict between their physical sex and their gender identity. Though the parents were relieved to understand what was happening, and agreed to stop trying to force Armand to live as a boy, they had another concern. By that time, Armand was eleven years old and getting close to puberty.

"We knew that puberty was around the corner, and we needed to start looking into [what to do]," Armand's father said. "How do we help this child . . . develop in a way that is consistent with who she is?"

Hormone Therapy to Redirect Puberty

Armand's parents learned about a radical treatment that had been used in similar situations to postpone puberty. It involved injections that would block **hormones** from being released in the body, effectively stopping sexual maturity.

"If you can block the gonads, that is the ovary or the testes, from making sex steroids, that being estrogen or testosterone, then you can literally prevent . . . almost all the physical differences between the genders,"

If sexual maturity and the development of secondary sex characteristics are postponed, males and females appear nearly indistinguishable.

says Norman Spack, an **endocrinologist** at Children's Hospital in Boston who was one of the first physicians to use this treatment in the United States. He notes that the process results in patients being infertile—unable to have children—due to damage done to the gonads.

In the second stage of the treatment, which occurs around age sixteen, the person can then choose to begin maturing sexually into their authentic gender by taking the appropriate hormones.

"We can make it possible that they can fit in in the way they want to," Spack says. "It is really quite amazing."

This is remarkably different from the difficulty and **trauma** of trying to fit in as a transgender adult, especially for men who develop male attributes such as height, a beard, an Adam's apple, large hands and feet, and other physical characteristics that are difficult to change when transitioning to a female as an adult.

Armand immediately chose to begin the treatments and started living full time as a girl named Violet. On her first day at school as a female, Violet nervously followed her parents into the school building.

"We said, 'No! You are not going to do this. You're not going to walk behind anybody,'" her father reported. "'We're going to walk together.' And we held hands and we marched right up the sidewalk into those doors."

Although Violet's school was supportive, teachers were afraid there might be teasing or even violence from other classmates. Nothing happened. The family said that after making the decision to allow Violet to transition, their lives became much happier and simpler.

Too Young to Be Certain?

Not everyone agrees that the therapy Violet underwent is the best course of action. Adolescence is a very confusing time for young people, and making the decision to transition can have a significant and lasting effect on their lives.

All of us have both masculine and feminine aspects of our personality, no matter what our sexual or gender identity is. This can become a problem for people when these aspects are so strongly out of sync with their biological sex that they are unable to feel that their own bodies express their true gender identity.

"You can have a child who is presenting with absolute certainty, but it may be that at a later point they will decide that is not in fact what they want and their feelings may indeed change," says Polly Carmichael, a British psychologist who works at the Portman Clinic in London. Young people enrolled in treatment at that clinic are required to live as the gender they were assigned at birth, and more than 80 percent opt to stay that sex in adulthood. However, researchers in the Netherlands, where the adolescent treatment was developed, have found that all the young people who chose to participate in their study remained transgender into adulthood.

Parental Concern ... and Confusion

Meg Clark has an eleven-year-old daughter who is transgender. During a time when many schoolchildren learn about sexuality and physical development, Clark noted that there were very limited resources for the information her daughter needed to help her development.

"Her whole class is separated by male and female on a special day to go to 'learning about your bodies,'" Clark said. "She's so sad she has none to go to."

Clark, like Violet's parents, accepts that her child is dealing with issues of sexual identity. But often, parents are confused when confronted with gender-variant children and try to force them to fit into traditional gender roles. This is frequently because they don't understand that there are alternatives. And, of course, they are naturally protective of their children and fear that others may subject them to teasing, harassment, and even violence because they are different.

Transgender issues are not unique to the modern Western world. In the past, in Asian cultures, being transgender was accepted and often respected.

"Being a parent of a gender-variant child can be really hard," says Dr. Laura Erickson-Schroth. "Most parents want to be understanding of their children, but they recognize that the world can be an unkind and even dangerous place for those who don't conform."

Erickson-Schroth edited *Trans Bodies, Trans Selves*, a book written by and for gender-variant people, specifically, adolescents and young adults with questions about their gender identity.

"I'd especially love for adolescents to read the section on transgender history, because all too often, generations of people are cut off from each other and prevented from coming together around common social and political goals," says Erickson-Schroth.

The Risks of Repressing Gender Identity

Forcing children to live according to standard gender roles will not change how they personally identify. And young people who recognize that they are gender variant may suffer depression, anxiety, and even suicidal thoughts if they are expected to deny their personal identity.

This is why education and understanding is so important. When someone identifies as a specific gender, it is most helpful to them to respect their personal identity. Friends and family members of gender-variant young people are often unsure how to proceed or what is expected of them. The most important thing is to listen and maintain an open mind.

Violet's sister Melina understood that if she wanted Violet to be happy, she had to try to imagine what it feels like to be transgender. She came to understand that feeling as if you are living in the wrong body can be frightening, confusing, and disturbing.

"To go through the process of the gender that you're really not … that must be the most scariest, most disgusting thing," says Melina. "I can't even imagine what that's like."

Violet's father, who has spent many years coming to accept his new daughter, now gets offended by people who think she was incapable of understanding her gender at such a young age.

"[They] say, 'Well, she's too young to know!' Well, when did you know you were a girl? When did I know I was a boy?" he says. "I knew my whole life. I can't tell you exactly when, but it wasn't like I was ten and realized, 'Oh gee, I must be a boy!' What people fail to realize is they made that decision way earlier than that. It just happened that their gender identity and their anatomy matched."

Among the organizations that advocate for transgender youth is TransActive, whose public service poster is shown here.

Violet is more fortunate than most trans adolescents; the acceptance of her parents and sister, and the strong base of support they offer, will make it easier for her to enter the outside world and live as a transgender adult.

CLOSE-UP: FINDING A TRANS COMMUNITY

There are numerous organizations available to provide support for transgender youth and their families.

- TransYouth Family Allies has an online support group for parents called TYFA Talk, and provides information for schools and healthcare providers. (www.imatyfa.org)

- TransFamily has an e-mail discussion group for parents as well as for children and teens. (www.transfamily.org)

- Gender Spectrum's website provides many health and human services resources, and even hosts events and support groups. (www.genderspectrum.org)

TEXT-DEPENDENT QUESTIONS

- Is childhood too early to have a fully formed transgender identity?

- How can parents and siblings best help a transgender child?

- Can gender identity change as a child moves through adolescence and adulthood?

 RESEARCH PROJECTS

- List some things you think might concern parents who learn they have a transgender child. Think about which of these are justified and which are based on prejudice or misinformation.

- If you know, or know of, a trans youth who's in your age range, ask about his or her journey.

- Make a list of the gender traits and qualities you'd like to express if you were to transition.

Comedian, actor, and writer Ian Harvie incorporates his life as a trans man into his stand-up performances. He co-starred in the award-winning Amazon series *Transparent*.

4.

LIVING AS A TRANSGENDER ADULT

Life in America has gotten **incrementally** better for transgender people. Every few months seems to bring some new indication of progress. One day, we find out that the Pentagon is preparing to end its policy prohibiting transgender Americans from serving in the military.

A little while after that, we learn that the *Diagnostic and Statistical Manual of Mental Disorders,* a kind of bible for mental health professionals, no longer includes the term *gender identity disorder,* opting to replace it with the far more neutral term *gender dysphoria.*

The Transgender Pride flag made its first public appearance at a pride parade in Phoenix in 2000. The flag's designer, Monica Helms, sought to represent the diversity of the transgender community, using light blue as the traditional color for baby boys, pink as the traditional color for baby girls, and white in the middle "for those who are transitioning, those who feel they have a neutral gender or no gender, and those who are intersexed."

These milestones are due at least in part to the increasing visibility of trans men and women in public life. By humanizing the trans experience, they make it relatable to the public.

Chaz Bono's openly transgender identity and advocacy efforts have helped bring acceptance and awareness to transgender issues. He is shown here with his partner Jennifer Elia.

Some trans celebrities became **prominent** after already having transitioned—such as Laverne Cox, a star of the Netflix series *Orange Is the New Black*. Others underwent the process very publicly, having already become well known in their original identity—such as Chaz Bono, who was the daughter of cultural icons Sonny and Cher and an outspoken advocate for LGBT rights.

Caitlyn Jenner is probably the most famous transgender figure in America today. Winner of the men's decathlon at the 1976 Summer Olympics, Jenner (then "Bruce") became an instant role model of triumphant American masculinity. Ironically, it was this celebrity that prevented her from transitioning to her true gender identity until middle age.

"I was growing up in a very different time, and I had no information," Caitlyn says. "Meanwhile, I had all of my diversions—sports … marriage … family—but after 65 years, here I was right back with the same problems that I had when I was ten years old, and I had to finally do something about it." Jenner's "doing something about it" resulted in a 2015 *Vanity Fair* profile with a glamorous cover portrait by celebrity photographer Annie Leibovitz, accompanied by a headline encouraging readers to "Call me Caitlyn." It was a milestone that would have been unimaginable even five years earlier, much less during Jenner's athletic prime.

The Downside of Acceptance

But new successes in trans rights carry with them a danger. As is true of most social movements, increasing visibility and acceptance can

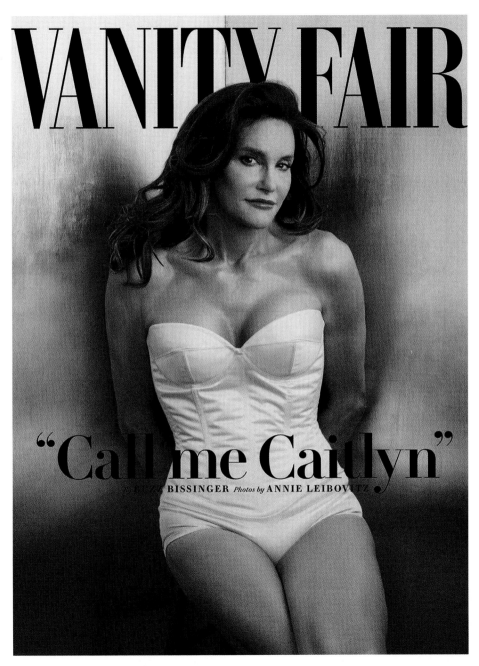

The groundbreaking July 2015 cover of *Vanity Fair* that introduced Caitlyn Jenner to the world.

also trigger a **backlash.** And trans people are more vulnerable to such attacks, on both a personal and institutional level.

Lack of employment protections for trans workers has resulted in an epidemic of trans unemployment; in most states, there are no laws prohibiting people from being fired because of their gender identity. As part of a congressional hearing, the Business Coalition for Workplace Fairness submitted a letter of support that said, in part:

To make our workplace values clear and transparent to our employees, customers and investors, each of our businesses have already implemented a non-discrimination policy, which is inclusive of gender identity and/or gender expression. This policy has been accepted broadly and we believe it has positively affected our bottom-line. Our philosophy and practice of valuing diversity encourages full and open participation by all employees. By treating all employees with fairness and respect we have been able to recruit and retain the best and brightest workers, thereby bringing a multitude of diverse opinions and perspectives to our organizations.

The statement was signed by dozens of supporting businesses that included Bank of America, Microsoft Corporation, General Motors Corporation, Eastman Kodak, Levi Strauss & Company, and Google Inc.

And yet, a recent National Transgender Discrimination Survey (NTDS) reveals that 47 percent of respondents reported either being fired, not hired, or denied promotion because they were transgender or gender nonconforming. The NTDS also reports a related fact: Fifteen percent of respondents were living in what they described as "severe poverty." In the Latino community, that figure shot up to 28 percent; for African Americans, it was a whopping 34 percent. Homelessness is a persistent trans problem as well, particularly for teenagers, who are often banished by their parents without any means of supporting themselves. Forty-one percent of trans teenagers have attempted suicide—an astronomical and tragic figure.

Changing the Way We Think About Transgender Individuals

Erickson-Schroth notes that some commonplace adjustments can be made to make environments more trans-friendly, such as having gender-neutral bathrooms and including "transgender" as an option on official forms, such as medical intake forms. This can make it easier for patients to address the topic with their doctors. Similarly, she suggests allowing space for a preferred name, in the event that a trans person prefers to be known as something other than his or her birth name.

Sadly, even such common-sense measures meet resistance; there is a slate of "bathroom bills" currently being proposed that would restrict trans people to using only public rest rooms that match the sex indicated on their birth certificates. And the inability to obtain accurate identity documents, such as driver's licenses, can adversely affect a trans person's life on many levels, including delaying and preventing access to public services. The Human Rights Campaign—the nation's largest lesbian, gay, bisexual, and transgender **advocacy** group—reports that many states require evidence of a medical transition, which not all trans people have had, or even desire.

But the situation is not all doom and gloom. Progress is being made. In June 2010, the U.S. State Department announced changes in policy guidelines regarding gender change on passports and other documents used by U.S. citizens when traveling abroad. The policy states that the gender listed on passports can be changed when documentation is provided from a medical doctor stating that the individual has undergone appropriate medical treatment for gender transition.

"We are grateful to the State Department for taking the necessary steps towards securing respectful treatment of transgender people who deserve to travel safely," said Dru Levasseur, Transgender Rights Attorney for Lambda Legal. "When traveling at home and abroad, transgender people have been subject to dangerous situations because their passports did not reflect their gender. These new guidelines will make travel safer for transgender people."

 CLOSE-UP: GENDER-NEUTRAL PRONOUNS

Some people don't identify as either male or female, which can cause problems when deciding which pronouns to use when addressing or speaking about them. If someone doesn't feel like a man or a woman, neither *he* nor *she* really describes who they are. Because English doesn't have any non-gendered pronouns, the genderqueer community has developed its own gender-neutral words. Many genderqueer individuals choose to go by the pronouns *ze/zir/zirs* (instead of *he/him/his* or *she/her/hers*), and this is probably the most popular alternative. Other gender-neutral pronouns that have been suggested include *thon/thons/thons, ve/ver/vis*, and *en/ens/ens*.

Members of the transgender community march through the streets of West Hollywood on November 20, 2015. Transgender Day of Remembrance is observed each year on this day to remember the victims of transphobia and to raise awareness of hate crimes committed against transgender individuals around the world.

Worth the Ongoing Struggle

For the time being, even navigating an average day can be a challenge for trans people. Cisgender people constantly make decisions and take actions based on their gender; it's so common, most never really think about it at all. But for transgender adults, the same situations can require many considerations and adjustments.

"It's interesting because when you really stop to think about it, gender is everywhere—using the restroom, shopping for clothing, even having casual conversations," says Helena Barrett, who assists transgender adults in finding health and human services. "Workplace dynamics can be challenging under ordinary circumstances. But for transgender people, it can be very complicated and even difficult, especially if people don't understand what it means or are ignorant about gender issues."

Despite all the difficulties that trans people face, from the trivial to the more consequential, you'll rarely hear a trans man or woman express regret about having transitioned. In fact, most will tell you enthusiastically that all the difficulties they've experienced pale before the sheer joy of finally being their own true, authentic selves.

TEXT-DEPENDENT QUESTIONS

- What are the positive and negative consequences of coming out as transgender?

- What can businesses do to help transgender employees succeed?

- Do trans people of different races face different challenges?

- Is there a time of life when it is too late to transition?

 RESEARCH PROJECTS

- Interview an older trans person about the process of transitioning to his or her true self.

- Visit the Transsexual Roadmap (tsroadmap.com), and examine the many different ways there are to transition.

- Visualize yourself a year after having transitioned … then five years … then ten.

📄 SERIES GLOSSARY

Activists: People committed to social change through political and personal action.

Advocacy: The process of supporting the rights of a group of people and speaking out on their behalf.

Alienation: A feeling of separation and distance from other people and from society.

Allies: People who support others in a cause.

Ambiguous: Something unclear or confusing.

Anonymous: Being unknown; having no one know who you are.

Assumption: A conclusion drawn without the benefit of real evidence.

Backlash: An adverse reaction by a large number of people, especially to a social or political development.

Bias: A tendency or preference toward a particular perspective or ideology that interferes with the ability to be impartial, unprejudiced, or objective.

Bigotry: Stubborn and complete intolerance of a religion, appearance, belief, or ethnic background that differs from one's own.

Binary: A system made up of two, and only two, parts.

Bohemian: Used to describe movements, people, or places characterized by nontraditional values and ways of life often coupled with an interest in the arts and political movements.

Caricature: An exaggerated representation of a person.

Celibate: Choosing not to have sex.

Chromosome: A microscopic thread of genes within a cell that carries all the information determining what a person is like, including his or her sex.

Cisgender: Someone who self-identifies with the gender he or she was assigned at birth.

Civil rights: The rights of a citizen to personal and political freedom under the law.

Clichés: Expressions that have become so overused—stereotypes, for example—that they tend to be used without thought.

Closeted: Choosing to conceal one's true sexual orientation or gender identity.

Compensating: Making up for something by trying harder or going further in the opposite direction.

Conservative: Cautious; resistant to change and new ideas.

Controversy: A disagreement, often involving a touchy subject about which differing opinions create tension and strong reactions.

Customs: Ideas and ways of doing things that are commonly understood and shared within a society.

Demonize: Portray something or someone as evil.

Denominations: Large groups of religious congregations united under a common faith and name, and organized under a single legal administration.

Derogatory: Critical or cruel, as in a term used to make a person feel devalued or humiliated.

Deviation: Something abnormal; something that has moved away from the standard.

Dichotomy: Division into two opposite and contradictory groups.

Discrimination: When someone is treated differently because of his or her race, sexual orientation, gender identity, religion, or some other factor.

Disproportionate: A situation where one particular group is overrepresented within a larger group.

Diverse: In the case of a community, one that is made up of people from many different backgrounds.

Effeminate: A word used to refer to men who have so-called feminine qualities.

Emasculated: Having had one's masculinity or manhood taken away.

Empathy: Feeling for another person; putting yourself mentally and emotionally in another person's place.

Empirical evidence: Factual data gathered from direct observation.

Empowering: Providing strength and energy; making someone feel powerful.

Endocrinologist: A medical doctor who specializes in the treatment of hormonal issues.

Epithets: Words or terms used in a derogatory way to put a person down.

The Establishment: The people who hold influence and power in society.

Extremist: Someone who is in favor of using extreme or radical measures, especially in politics and religion.

Flamboyant: Colorful and a bit outrageous.

Fundamentalist: Someone who believes in a particular religion's fundamental principles and follows them rigidly. When the word is used in connection with Christianity, it refers to a member of a form of Protestant Christianity that believes in the strict and literal interpretation of the Bible.

Gay liberation: The movement for the civil and legal rights of gay people that originated in the 1950s and emerged as a potent force for social and political change in the late 1960s and '70s.

Gender: A constructed sexual identity, whether masculine, feminine, or entirely different.

Gender identity: A person's self-image as female, male, or something entirely different, no matter what gender a person was assigned at birth.

Gender roles: Those activities and traits that are considered appropriate to males and females within a given culture.

Gene: A microscopic sequence of DNA located within a chromosome that determines a particular biological characteristic, such as eye color.

Genitalia: The scientific term for the male and female sex organs.

Genocide: The large-scale murder and destruction of a particular group of people.

Grassroots: At a local level; usually used in reference to political action that begins within a community rather than on a national or global scale.

Harassed/harassment: Being teased, bullied, or physically threatened.

Hate crime: An illegal act in which the victim is targeted because of his or her race, religion, sexual orientation, or gender identity.

Homoerotic: Having to do with homosexual, or same-sex, love and desire.

Homophobia: The fear and hatred of homosexuality. A homophobic person is sometimes referred to as a "homophobe."

Horizontal hostility: Negative feeling among people within the same minority group.

Hormones: Chemicals produced by the body that regulate biological functions, including male and female gender traits, such as beard growth and breast development.

Identity: The way a person, or a group of people, defines and understands who they are.

Inborn: Traits, whether visible or not, that are a part of who we are at birth.

Inclusive: Open to all ideas and points of view.

Inhibitions: Feelings of guilt and shame that keep us from doing things we might otherwise want to do.

Internalized: Taken in; for example, when a person believes the negative opinions other people have of him, he has *internalized* their point of view and made it his own.

Interpretation: A particular way of understanding something.

Intervention: An organized effort to help people by changing their attitudes or behavior.

Karma: The force, recognized by both Hindus and Buddhists, that emanates from one's actions in this life; the concept that the good and bad things one does determine where he or she will end up in the next life.

Legitimized: Being taken seriously and having the support of large numbers of people.

LGBT: An initialism that stands for lesbian, gay, bisexual, and transgender. Sometimes a "Q" is added (**LGBTQ**) to include "questioning." "Q" may also stand for "queer."

Liberal: Open to new ideas; progressive; accepting and supportive of the ideas or identity of others.

Liberation: The act of being set free from oppression and persecution.

Mainstream: Accepted, understood, and supported by the majority of people.

Malpractice: When a doctor or other professional gives bad advice or treatment, either out of ignorance or deliberately.

Marginalize: Push someone to the sidelines, away from the rest of the world.

Mentor: Someone who teaches and offers support to another, often younger, person.

Monogamous: Having only one sexual or romantic partner.

Oppress: Keep another person or group of people in an inferior position.

Ostracized: Excluded from the rest of a group.

Out: For an LGBT person, the state of being open with other people about his or her sexual orientation or gender identity.

Outed: Revealed or exposed as LGBT against one's will.

Persona: A character or personality chosen by a person to change the way others perceive them.

Pioneers: People who are the first to try new things and experiment with new ways of life.

Politicized: Aware of one's rights and willing to demand them through political action.

Prejudice: An opinion (usually unfavorable) of a person or a group of people not based on actual knowledge.

Proactive: Taking action taken in advance of an anticipated situation or difficulty.

Progressive: Supporting human freedom and progress.

Psychologists and psychiatrists: Professionals who study the human mind and human behavior. Psychiatrists are medical doctors who can prescribe pills, whereas clinical psychologists provide talk therapy.

Quackery: When an untrained person gives medical advice or treatment, pretending to be a doctor or other medical expert.

The Right: In politics and religion, the side that is generally against social change and new ideas; often used interchangeably with *conservative*.

Segregation: Historically, a system of laws and customs that limited African Americans' access to many businesses, public spaces, schools, and neighborhoods that were "white only."

Sexual orientation: A person's physical and emotional attraction to the opposite sex (heterosexuality), the same sex (homosexuality), both sexes (bisexuality), or neither (asexuality).

Sociologists: People who study the way groups of humans behave.

Spectrum: A wide range of variations.

Stereotype: A caricature; a way to judge someone, probably unfairly, based on opinions you may have about a particular group they belong to.

Stigma: A mark of shame.

Subculture: A smaller group of people with similar interests and lifestyles within a larger group.

Taboo: Something that is forbidden.

Theories: Ideas or explanations based on research, experimentation, and evidence.

Tolerance: Acceptance of, and respect for, other people's differences.

Transgender: People who identify with a gender different from the one they were assigned at birth.

Transphobia: Fear or hatred of transgender people.

Variance: A range of differences within a category such as gender.

Victimized: Subjected to unfair and negative treatment, including violence, bullying, harassment, or prejudice.

FURTHER RESOURCES

National Center for Transgender Equality
The nation's leading social justice advocacy organization of transgender people.
www.transequality.org

Human Rights Campaign
The country's largest LGBT civil rights advocacy group and political lobbying organization.
www.hrc.com

PFLAG
A support group formerly known as Parents, Families and Friends of Lesbians and Gays.
www.community.pflag.org

Trans Youth Family Allies
Raises public awareness of the challenges faced by children with gender-variant identities.
www.imatyfa.org

Trans Lifeline
Hotline staffed by transgender volunteers providing support to the transgender community. United States: (877) 565-8860; Canada: (877) 330-6366.
www.translifeline.org

The Williams Institute
A think-tank at UCLA Law dedicated to independent research on sexual orientation and gender identity law and public policy.
williamsinstitute.law.ucla.edu/category/research/transgender-issues

Gender Spectrum
Works to create gender-sensitive and inclusive environments for all children and teens.
www.genderspectrum.org

Girls Are… Boys Are…: Myths, Stereotypes & Gender Differences
An in-depth examination of these issues released by the Office of Educational Research and Improvement, U.S. Department of Education.
www.campbell-kibler.com/Stereo.pdf

Transsexual Roadmap
A "travel guide" designed to help set priorities and choose the route of one's transition.
www.tsroadmap.com

Gender Talk: Speaking the Language of Gender
News, information, and references about transgenderism, crossdressing, and transsexualism.
www.gendertalk.com

INDEX

advocacy 16, 31, 41, 45, 47–48, 51, 53,
ambiguity 11, 17
androgynous 25

"bathroom bills" 51

cisgender 24, 53,
crossdresser 23, 27, 29

Diagnostic and Statistical Manual of Mental Disorders
    45–46
drag 23, 27–28
  king 23, 27
  queen 23, 27–28

effeminate 11, 16, 24
endocrinologist 33, 35

female 11, 13–14, 17–21, 25, 28–30, 35–36,
    38, 52
feminine 11, 14, 17, 37

gay 15–16, 23, 27, 30, 46, 51
gender 11, 17, 24, 26–29, 35, 38, 40, 52–54
  binary systems 11, 17, 25
  characteristics 12, 15
  identity 20, 23–24, 27, 29–30, 33, 37, 39–40,
    48, 50
  nonconformity 19, 32
  prejudice 17
  programming 20
  roles 13–19, 24, 38, 40,
  variant 23–24, 38–40
gender dysphoria 46
gender identity disorder 34, 46

Gender Spectrum 42
genderqueer 23, 25, 52

hermaphrodite 28
hormone therapy 34–36
Human Rights Campaign 51

intersex 23, 28–29

Lambda Legal 52
LGBT 23–24, 48

male 11, 14, 16–21, 25, 27–29, 34–36, 38, 52
masculine 13, 17, 24, 37

pronouns 52

sex 12–14, 17–18, 20–21, 25, 27, 29, 35, 37–38, 51
  characteristics 15, 35
sexual identity 37–38
sexuality 14–16, 32, 38
spectrum 23, 25–26
stereotype 23, 27
straight 16, 27, 30

TransActive 41
Trans Bodies, Trans Selves 39
Transexual Roadmap 25
TransFamily 42
transgender 14, 19, 23, 24–25, 27, 29–30, 32,
    36, 38–41, 45–46, 48, 50–52, 54
  identity 47
transition 29, 36, 48, 51–52, 54
transvestite 23, 27
TransYouth Family Allies 42